S0-BZD-693

May I Come In ?

THEODORE CLYMER · DORIS GATES

CONSULTANTS

ROGER W. SHUY · E. PAUL TORRANCE
LINGUISTICS   CREATIVITY

GINN AND COMPANY

A XEROX COMPANY

Acknowledgments

Grateful acknowledgment is made to the following authors and publishers for permission to use and adapt copyrighted materials:

Curtis Publishing Company for "Mr. Big," adapted from "The Little Old Man and His Farm" by Edna Geries. Reprinted by special permission from JACK AND JILL © 1964 The Curtis Publishing Company.

E. P. Dutton & Co., Inc., for "Timothy Boon." From the book FAIRIES AND SUCHLIKE by Ivy O. Eastwick. Copyright, 1946, by E. P. Dutton & Co., Inc. Reprinted by permission of the publishers.

Golden Press, Inc., for "Bozo." Adapted by permission from TOO MANY BOZOS by Lillian Moore. © Copyright 1960 by Golden Press, Inc. Also "Home for a Bunny." Reprinted by permission from HOME FOR A BUNNY by Margaret Wise Brown. Copyright © 1956, 1961 by Golden Press, Inc.

Grosset & Dunlap, Inc., for "Mr. Pine's Signs" and "The Mixed-Up Signs." Adaptation of MR. PINE'S MIXED-UP SIGNS, by Leonard Kessler, Copyright © 1961 by Wonder Books, a division of Grosset & Dunlap, Inc., by permission of the publisher, Wonder Books, a division of Grosset & Dunlap, Inc.

Harcourt, Brace & World, Inc., for "Buildings." From WHISPERS AND OTHER POEMS, © 1958 by Myra Cohn Livingston. Reprinted by permission of Harcourt, Brace & World, Inc.

Harper & Row, Publishers for reprinting "The Giant" from ALL THAT SUNLIGHT by Charlotte Zolotow. Copyright © 1967 by Charlotte Zolotow. Reprinted with permission of Harper & Row.

J. B. Lippincott Company for "About the Teeth of Sharks" from YOU READ TO ME, I'LL READ TO YOU by John Ciardi. Copyright © 1962 The Curtis Publishing Company. Published by J. B. Lippincott Company.

G. P. Putnam's Sons for "Whistles." Reprinted by permission of G. P. Putnam's Sons from HERE, THERE AND EVERYWHERE by Dorothy Aldis. Copyright 1927, 1928 by Dorothy Aldis.

To Catherine Woolley for use of the idea for "Mr. Cunningham" from the story "Mr. Cunningham" by Jane Thayer, copyright © 1955 by Humpty Dumpty, Inc.

Child Life and Elizabeth Touchette for ideas used in "Out in Space" and suggested by "The Martian Who Lost His Oo" by Elizabeth Touchette in *Child Life* magazine, January, 1966.

Illustrators: Marilyn Bass, Willi Baum, Tom Cooke, Lois Ehlert, George Guzzi, John Kuzich, Jerry Pinkney, Donald Silverstein, Lynn Sweat, Joseph Veno, Jean Winslow, Fred Witzig

© COPYRIGHT, 1969, BY GINN AND COMPANY

ALL RIGHTS RESERVED

HOME OFFICE, BOSTON, MASSACHUSETTS 02117

Contents

Animals

In the City

All for Fun

Boys and Girls

Old Tales

BOOK-LENGTH STORY

Home for a Bunny, MARGARET WISE BROWN

ANIMALS

ELEPHANTS AT WORK

A man and a big elephant
are working here.
What work are they doing ?

6

This elephant is working, too.

It is working with big logs.

What will the elephant do

with the logs ?

A big elephant is helping this man.
What is the elephant doing?

8

A man wants to ride on this elephant.

A boy is helping the man

get on the elephant.

Who will ride with the man?

What work can elephants do?

What animals live here ?

What animals live here ?

What animals live here ?

What animals live here ?

A surprise for Pat

"Mother, come here," said Pat.
"See the rabbits in the snow."

"They are looking for something
to eat," said Mother.

Pat said, "What can they find
in the snow?
Can't we find something
for the rabbits to eat?"

14

Mother said, "What food do rabbits like to eat?"

"Here's something they like," said Pat.

"We can surprise the rabbits with this food."

Pat put the food on the snow.

"The rabbits ran away,"
he said.

"Will they come and eat here?
Will they find the food I put
on the snow?"

" We will see, " said Mother.

" Don't you want to put food
in the tree, too ? "

" In the tree ? " said Pat.

" Rabbits don't live in trees ! "

" No, they don't, " said Mother.

" But you can put food in the tree.

And we will see who finds it. "

Pat said,

" Mother ! Mother !
Come and see the rabbits.
They are eating the food
on the snow. "

" Yes, they are, " said Mother.
" Look in the tree, Pat.
Who is eating the food you put
in the tree ? "

" A raccoon ! " said Pat.
" He's eating in the tree.
I surprised the rabbits.
The raccoon surprised me. "

THE Raccoons

Little raccoons live
in this home.
They live with Mother Raccoon.

The little raccoons can't see.
They can't play.
They are too little to go
away from home.

Now the little raccoons can see.

Now they can play.

And they can go away from home.

They follow Mother Raccoon.

The little raccoons go

down the tree.

Down they go with Mother Raccoon.

They follow Mother Raccoon

away from the tree.

The little raccoons like to play.

They run up and down the hill.

Now the little raccoons are going home.
They follow Mother Raccoon up the tree.

22

Now the little raccoons can go
away from the hill.

They follow Mother Raccoon.

The raccoons want something
to eat.

What can they find here?

Now the raccoons are too old
to live with Mother Raccoon.

They are too big for the home
in the tree.

The raccoons are looking
for food.

What can they find here ?

24

What animal ran
up the hill
in the snow?

and you will know.

Follow the tracks, **TRACKS in the snow**

25

What animal ran
on the hill
in the snow?

Follow the tracks, and you will know.

What animal ran
down the hill
in the snow?

Follow the tracks, and you will know.

27

Look in the homes, and you will know

28

who made the tracks
you see in the snow.

29

ANIMALS IN DANGER

Some animals can hide from danger.

Can you see the fawn?

Can you see the squirrel?   Can you see the bear?

30

Some animals can get away from danger.

What can raccoons do?

What can ducks do?

What can a frog do?

31

THE SQUIRREL

Whisky, frisky,
Hippity hop,
Up he goes
To the

tree

top!

Whirly,
twirly,
Round and round,
Down he scampers
To the ground.

32

Furly,
curly,

What a tail !

Tall as a feather,

Broad as a sail !

Where's his supper ?

In the shell.

Snappity,

crackity, Out it fell !

Author Unknown

33

Can You Read This?

at	tracks	Dad	Nan
Pat	back	Lad	ran
fat	sack	mad	tan
rat		bad	fan

Is the raccoon fat?

Is the elephant tan?

Can a fox eat a rat?

Did this bear want a fan?

Is the elephant mad?

Can a goat hide in a sack?

Reinforcing decoding: Direct the pupils to decode each of the words at the top. Then they may read the questions and answer them from picture clues.

34

What Animal Is This?

What Animal Is Like This?

Reinforcing literal comprehension: Direct the pupils to identify the animals and compare them with related pictures at the right.

What Is in the Tree?

cap can
cat
sat
Pat

mad map man
Lad
Dad

ham had
hat
bat
Pat

bat bag
bad
mad
Dad

tag tap
tan
can
ran

sat Sam
sad
Lad
Dad

Reinforcing decoding: Direct the pupils to read each "tree trunk" from the bottom up, and then "go out on a limb."

36

IN THE CITY

NEW BOOTS

James said, " I want new boots.
Do you have boots for boys ? "

" Yes, we do, " said the man.
" Come with me, and you can see
what we have. "

James said, "I have some old boots
at home.

But they are too little for me."

"We want boots James can put on,"
said Mother.

"We can find some boots for James,"
said the man.

"We will find boots he can put on."

James and Mother looked at boots
for boys.

James put on some big boots.
He said, " Here are the boots I want.
Mother, will you get the boots
for me ? "

" Yes, I will, "
said Mother.

Penny said,
" Will you get
new boots
for me, too ? "

" No, Penny, "
said Mother.

" The boots you have are not old.
I don't want to get new boots
for you now. "

The man said,
"Here is a balloon
for you.
It comes
with the new boots."

"Thank you,"
said James.

He looked at Penny.
"I have some new boots," he said.
"Do you want this balloon?"

"Yes, I do," said Penny.
"Now I have something new!
Thank you, James."

James said,
" I like my new boots. "

the
red
balloon

Penny said,
" I like my red balloon, too. "

"Don't play with the balloon
in here," said Mother.
"You can play with it at home."

Mother and James went on.
They did not see where Penny went.

"Hello, little dog,"
said Penny.
"Do you like
my red balloon?"

The dog surprised Penny.
He surprised the woman, too.

Penny said, "Stop! Stop!
Where are you going
with my balloon?"

The woman said, " Stop, Jet.
You come here ! "

Jet did not stop.
He ran fast.

Penny said, " My balloon !
The dog can't have it. "

The woman went to get Jet.

But she did not know
where to look.

" The woman is looking
for the balloon, " said Mother.

" She wants to get it for you. "

" She wants Jet, " said Penny.

" But I want my red balloon. "

46

WHERE IS JET?

Mother and James went with Penny
to look for Jet.

But they did not see the little dog.

A man asked, " Are you looking
for something ? "

" Yes, we are, " said Mother.
" We are looking for a dog
with a red balloon. "

47

" A dog ? " asked the man.

" A dog with a balloon ? "

" Can you help find the dog ? "
asked Penny.

" We don't know where he went. "

" I know ! " said James.

" Look, Mother.

I see Jet. "

48

The woman saw Jet, too.

But Penny saw the balloon.
She said, " My balloon !
Now I can't play with it. "

Mother said, " We can get
a new balloon, Penny. "

" We have some animal balloons, "
said the man.

" Animal balloons ? " asked Penny.
" I like animal balloons. "

The woman said,
" Let me get
a balloon
for Penny. "

50

Penny looked at the animal balloons,
and she saw a parrot.
She saw a big
purple parrot.

The woman asked,
" Do you want
the purple
balloon ?

You may have it, Penny. "

" Thank you, " said Penny.
" Now I have a parrot.
And you have Jet. "

A RIDE IN THE PARK

Dandy and the policeman went
to the park.

The policeman said, " Stop, Dandy.
This boy may want help. "

The policeman looked down.
He said, " Hello.
Are you lost ? "

" No, " said the boy.
" I'm not lost.
My mother is lost. "

The policeman asked, " Who are you ? "

" I'm Pete, " said the boy.
" I don't know where my mother is.
She's lost in this park. "

" Dandy and I will help you, Pete, "
said the policeman.
" Do you want to ride with me ? "

" Oh, can I ? " asked Pete.

" Up you go, " said the policeman.

Pete said, " I like to ride on Dandy.
I like to ride with you, too. "

" Are you looking, Pete ? "
asked the policeman.

" Yes, I'm looking, " said Pete.
" But I can't see my mother. "

" Don't stop looking, "
said the policeman.

" Mother ! Mother ! " said Pete.

" Look at me ! "

" Where did you go ? " asked Mother.

" I lost you, Pete. "

" Oh, I did not get lost, " said Pete.

" The policeman let me ride
on Dandy.

We looked for you, Mother. "

The policeman said, " Dandy and I
like to help boys.

We like to help lost mothers, too. "

THE BIG MACHINE

James said, " Ken and I want to go down the street.

We want to see the big machine. "

Mother said, " I don't want you to go down the street.

You can see the machine from here. "

" I like to see the machine, "
said James.

" But I want to play.
Let's do something, Ken.
I know ! Let's make a machine. "

Ken said, " Let's make it
at my house. "

" Mother, can I go to Ken's house ? "
asked James.

" Yes, you may, " said Mother.
" But don't go down the street. "

57

The boys ran up the street
to Ken's house.
They looked for some boxes and a ball.

James said, " We have big boxes
and little boxes.
The boxes are the houses, Ken.
And the ball is the machine. "

Ken said, "The houses are up.
Now make the machine work."

"Here it comes,"
said James.

James did not see Mop.
But Ken did.

"No, Mop!" said Ken.

"Don't run here!"

But Mop did not stop.

James said, " The machine worked !
It worked, Ken.
The houses are down. "

" Look at Mop run, " said Ken.
" He helped.

He made *the* *houses* *come* *down.* "

Buildings *Myra Cohn Livingston*

Buildings are a great surprise,
Every one's a different size.
            Offices
               Grow
                  long
                     and
                        high,
                           tall
                        enough
                              to
                           touch
                        the
                        sky.

Houses
   seem
more like a box,
made of glue
and building blocks.
Every time you look,
   you see
      Buildings
         shaped quite
            differently.

61

Old Buildings and New

Men are working in the city.
They want to take down
some old buildings.

The men work with big machines,
and the old buildings come down.

Now the old buildings are down,
and new buildings are going up.

Men work with machines here, too.
Up go the new buildings.

Men work to finish
the new buildings.
They work with machines.

Now some men are working
in this new building.

They will finish the building,
and people will come here to live.

Machines That Help You Work

What can you do with these machines ?

pencil sharpener   can opener   telephone dial

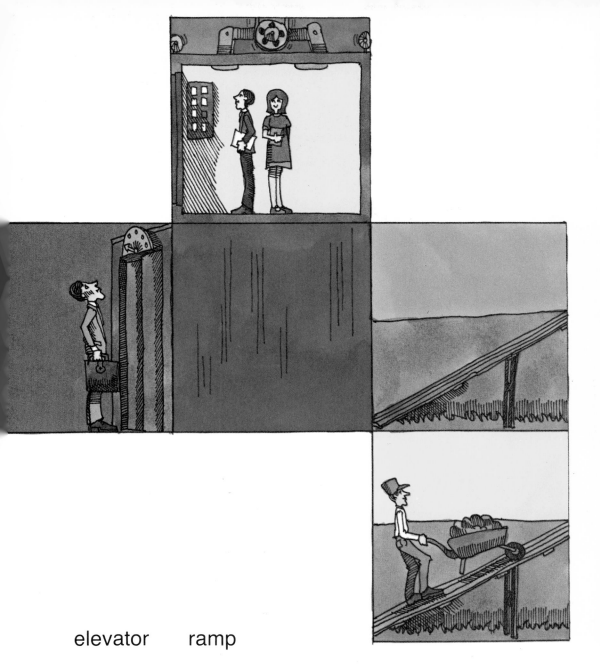

elevator   ramp

Cross Words

```
     | n |              |  l  |
-----+---+-----    -----+-----+-----
  p  |   |  t        z  |     |  p
-----+---+-----    -----+-----+-----
     | t |              |  d  |
```

```
     | t |              |  w  |
-----+---+-----    -----+-----+-----
  c  |   |  n        f  |     |  d
-----+---+-----    -----+-----+-----
     | g |              |  t  |
```

```
     | s |              |  f  |
-----+---+-----    -----+-----+-----
  r  |   |  p        p  |     |  g
-----+---+-----    -----+-----+-----
     | d |              |  t  |
```

Reinforcing decoding: Have the pupils choose the letter <u>a</u>, <u>e</u>, or <u>i</u> to make two meaningful words.

68

Triplets

ten tan tin	means 10
lad led lid	is a boy, not a man
pat pit pet	may be a dog or a cat
bid bed bad	is to take a nap in
pen pin pan	is something to put food in

mass miss mess	is a woman, not a man
pick pack peck	to put in a bag
big beg bag	to ask and ask
bit bet bat	to hit a ball
sit sat set	may be ten things

Reinforcing decoding: Have each word in a box read. Let pupils decide which one of the "triplets" is related to each phrase that follows.

69

What Machine Is This?

What Machine Is Like This?

Recognizing analogies: Direct the pupils to identify the machines and compare them with related pictures at right

70

ALL FOR FUN

"I want to sleep," said Mr. Big.
"Go away and let me sleep."

Did the animals go away?
No, they did not.

The goat said, "Ma-a-a!"
The duck said, "Quack! Quack!"
The cow said, "Moo-oo! Moo-oo!"

72

Mr. Big said, "I can't sleep here,
but I know what I can do.
I'm going to the city.
Now!"

The animals saw Mr. Big go away.
"Ma-a-a! Ma-a-a!" said the goat.
"Quack! Quack!" said the duck.
"Moo-oo! Moo-oo!" said the cow.

73

Away went Mr. Big.

"I want to see the new buildings,"
he said.

"I can walk up and down the streets.
And I can walk in the park.
I'm going to sleep in the city, too."

74

Mr. Big saw some new buildings.

He walked up and down the streets,
and he walked in the park.

"Now I want to sleep," said Mr. Big.

"My animals can't stop me
from sleeping in the city."

HOTEL
→

75

Did Mr. Big go to sleep?
No, he did not.

" Who can sleep in this city ? "
he asked.
" I can't!
Not with cars going up and down
the streets.
The cars come and go, and
they don't stop. "

76

John Kuzich

Mr. Big said, " I'm going home.
I will get my car and go now."

He walked down the street.
And away he went.

The animals ran to Mr. Big,
but he did not stop.

" I'm going to sleep, " he said.
" Now ! "

The goat said, " Ma-a-a ! Ma-a-a ! "
The duck said, " Quack ! Quack ! "
The cow said, " Moo-oo ! Moo-oo ! "

Did Mr. Big get up ?
No, he did not.
Mr. Big went to sleep.

78

Carlo looked down the street.

He said, " Mr. Babbit is sleeping.
I'm going to the park.
Mr. Babbit is in bed,
and he can't stop me. "

Mr. Boots said, " Hello, Carlo.

Where is Mr. Babbit ? "

Carlo went on.

Away he ran.

Mr. Boots said, " Stop, Carlo !
Don't run away.
You will get lost. "

But Carlo did not stop.

A woman said, " Hello, Carlo.
Here is something
for you. "

Carlo ran on.

He ran fast.

" Stop, Carlo ! Stop ! " said the woman.
"Don't run away. "

But Carlo did not stop.

"Get out of the street!"
said a policeman.
"You can't run here.
Get out of the street fast."

Carlo ran to the park.

He did not stop.

"I'm going to eat in the park,"
said Carlo.

A man looked up.

He said, "You can't eat here.

Go away!"

Carlo ran away from the man.

He ran to a tree, and up he went.

Carlo looked down from the tree.
He saw the man working.

He saw some boys playing.

Carlo wanted to play, too.
It was fun to run
away from home.
But it was not fun
without Mr. Babbit.

Mr. Babbit was not in bed.
He was in the park
looking for Carlo.

Mr. Babbit looked up
and said, "Carlo!
What are you doing
in the tree?
You come down."

And Carlo did.
He jumped on Mr. Babbit.
And away they went.

85

Timothy Boon
Bought a balloon
Blue as the sky,
Round as the moon.
" Now I will try
To make it fly
Up to the moon,
Higher than high ! "
Timothy said,
Nodding his head.

Timothy Boon
Sent his balloon
Up through the skies,
Up to the moon.

But a strong breeze
Stirred in the trees,
Rocked the bright moon,
Tossed the great seas,
And, with its mirth,
Shook the whole earth.

Timothy Boon,
And his balloon,
Caught by the breeze
Flew to the moon;
Up past the trees,
Over the seas,
Up to the moon —
Swift as you please ! —
And, ere I forget,
They have not come down yet !

Ivy O. Eastwick

OUT IN SPACE

Nog saw the space ship come down.
" Here comes Doodle, " he said.
" Don't you want to see Doodle ? "

Nog ran to the space ship.

88

Wig ran to see Doodle.

She said, " We looked for you.

Where did you go ? "

" Out in space, " said Doodle.

" In space ? " asked Nog.

" Oh, Doodle ! " said Wig.

" What did you see ? "

" I saw people, " said Doodle.

Nog said, " People !
Doodle saw people. "

" What are people like ? " asked Wig.
" What do they do ? "

Doodle said, " People are funny.
They do funny things.
They live in boxes. "

" Oh, no ! " said Wig.
" Not in boxes ! "

90

" I saw things that looked like bugs, "
said Doodle.

" Bugs ! " said Nog.
" Doodle saw bugs. "

" Some people ride in bugs, " said Doodle.

" Oh, no ! " said Wig.
" Not in bugs ! "

91

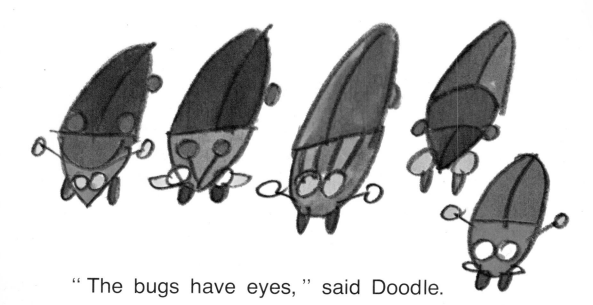

" The bugs have eyes, " said Doodle.

" Some eyes are red,
and some are yellow. "

" Eyes ! " said Nog.

" Doodle saw bugs
with red and yellow eyes. "

Wig said, " I want to go
out in space, too.

I want to see all the things
you saw, Doodle.

Will you take me ? "

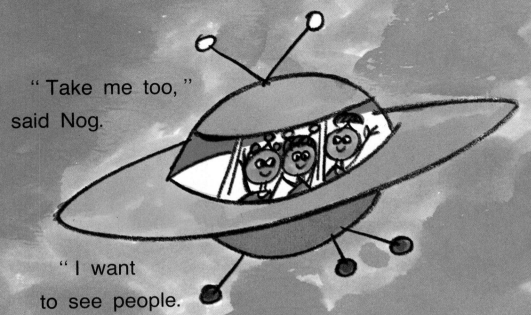

" Take me too, "
said Nog.

" I want
to see people.
And boxes.
And bugs.
Bugs with red eyes
and bugs with yellow eyes. "

" Let's go ! " said Doodle.

And   away   they   went—

Doodle,

Nog,

and Wig.

Let's Imagine Funny Things

What funny things do you see here ?

Can you imagine
    a hen with a pen ?
    a cat who can bat ?
    a pig with a wig ?

What funny things can you think of ?
    a fox in a _____ ?
    a goat in a _____ ?
    a _____ with a _____ ?

95

Mr. Pine's Signs

Mr. Pine made signs.

He made signs that said Stop.

He made signs that said Go.

Mr. Pine made all of the signs in Little Town.

He made signs for the streets.

And he made signs for the buildings.

96

The people in Little Town
liked the signs he made.

But the signs in Little Town got old.
They got too old for the people to read.

The Mayor said, " I will ask Mr. Pine
to make some new signs. "

And the Mayor went to find Mr. Pine.

"The signs are too old for people
to read," said the Mayor.
"Will you make new signs for Little Town?"

"Yes, I will," said Mr. Pine.
"And I can put up the signs, too."

The Mayor went home,
and Mr. Pine went to work.

Mr. Pine made red signs,
and green signs, and yellow signs.

A red sign said Stop.
A green sign said Park.
A yellow sign said Hill Street.

" Now the signs are all made, "
said Mr. Pine.
" And I'm going to sleep. "

Mr. Pine got up and said,
" Now where did I put
my glasses ? "

He looked and looked.

" I can't find my glasses, "
he said.
" That's funny !
I don't know where they are. "

100

Mr. Pine
looked here.

And here.

And here.

" I can't stop to find my glasses, "
said Mr. Pine.

" I have to put up the new signs. "

He got the signs
and went out of the house.

102

The Mixed-Up Signs

Mr. Pine put up all of the signs.

He did not know

they were mixed up.

But they were!

The signs in the streets
looked funny.
They were all mixed up !

A man said, "What is this?"

A woman said, "Oh, no!"

The policeman said, "Who did this?"

The Mayor said, "Find Mr. Pine. Fast!"

"All the signs are up,"
said Mr. Pine.

"And I can look for my glasses.
Now where are they?"

He looked and looked.

"Did I put my glasses in here?"
he asked.

Mr. Pine looked in the dog house.

He said, " My glasses !

Here they are. "

Mr. Pine put the glasses on

and went to see the signs.

This is what Mr. Pine saw.

" Oh, my ! " said Mr. Pine.

" My signs are all mixed up. "

" Mr. Pine ! Mr. Pine ! "
said the Mayor.

" Do something !
Fix the signs ! "

Mr. Pine went to work.
He fixed all the signs in Little Town.

The signs are not mixed up now.

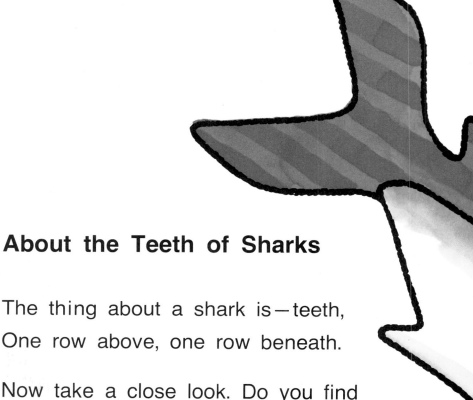

About the Teeth of Sharks

The thing about a shark is — teeth,
One row above, one row beneath.

Now take a close look. Do you find
It has another row behind ?

Still closer — here, I'll hold your hat:
Has it a third row behind that ?

Now look in and . . . Look out ! Oh my,
I'll *never* know now ! Well, goodbye.

John Ciardi

110

111

Can You Find It?

Pat has a   jam

Sam wants some   pack

Dan gets a   hat

Jack has a   pan

Reinforcing decoding: Have the children finish each sentence with the word that has the same ending as the underlined word in the sentence.

What Color Did You Say?

yellow red purple green black

blue white brown orange

Is this duck blue?

Do you think white is the right color for a machine?

Can you think what made the queen green?

Is a cow purple? Do you want to be one?

Is a house black?

What color is this thing?

Learning the color words: Have the color words identified with the splotches of color. Then the questions may be read and answered.

Steps

trick

quick

six

mix

fix

wake

take

rake

make

lake

cake

bake

tray

play

say

Ray

pay

may

lay

Kay

hay

day

Reinforcing decoding: Have the steps read from bottom to top.

114

BOYS AND GIRLS

Time for Bed

Jen said, "It's time for bed.

I can't sleep when you boys are playing in here.

When are you going to bed?"

"We don't want to sleep," said Ken.

"Pete and I want to have some fun."

Pete said, "Get down, Mop. Get down."

"Look out, Pete!" said Jen.

And down went Mop.

116

" What are you boys doing ? "
asked Dad.

" Do you know what time it is ? "

" What are you doing in here ? "
asked Mother.

" It's late, Jen. "

" I know it's late, " said Jen.

" But the boys are not in bed.

I can't sleep when they are playing. "

" It's time to stop playing, "
said Dad.

" Go to bed, boys. "

" I will, " said Pete.

Dad said, " In you go, Pete.
Don't get out of bed this time. "

Mother said, " Go to sleep, boys.
Come with me, Jen. "

" Good night, Pete, " said Jen.

" Good night, Dad and Ken. "

Pete looked up.

He said, " Good night, Jen.

Good night, Ken. "

Ken looked down.

He said, " Good night, Mop.

Good night, Pop. "

" Good night ! " said Dad.

" Now we can all go to sleep. "

I want to learn to whistle.
I've always wanted to.
I fix my mouth to do it, but
The whistle won't come through.

I think perhaps it's stuck, and so
I try it once again.
Can people swallow whistles?
Where is my whistle then ?

Dorothy Aldis

Pete Wants to Whistle

Pete said, " I want to whistle, but I can't.

Will you help me ? "

" Not now, " said Jen.

" I want to jump. "

" All you do is jump, " said Pete.

" You jump all the time ! "

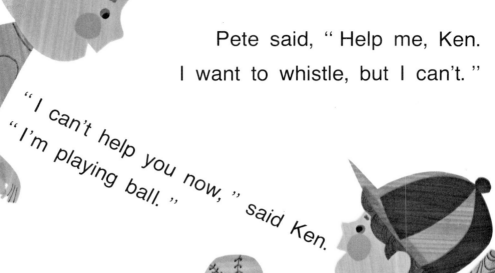

Pete said, " Help me, Ken.
I want to whistle, but I can't. "

" I can't help you now, " said Ken.
" I'm playing ball. "

" You play all the time ! "
said Pete.
" Who will help me ? "

Ken said, " Ask Dad.
He can whistle. "

122

Pete went to find Dad.
He said, " I want to whistle.
Will you help me ? "

Dad said, " Look here, Pete.
Do what I'm doing. "

" I am doing what you do, " said Pete.
" But I can't whistle. "

" Some time you will, " said Dad.

123

Pete said, " I want to shave, too. "

" No, Pete, " said Dad.
" You can't shave.
Put the can down. "

But it was too late.
Something came out of the can.
It came out fast.

" Wh-wh-wh ! " said Pete.

" Wh-wh-wh ! "

He looked up and said, " I whistled !
I whistled, Dad. "

" Yes, you did, " said Dad.
" That was a good whistle. "

" I went wh-wh-wh, " said Pete,
" and the whistle came out. "

Fun Around Home

Red light!

Green light!

Look what I made!

Teddy bear, teddy bear,
Turn around,
Teddy bear, teddy bear,
Touch the ground.

He's out!

One, two, three, four, five,
six, seven, eight, nine, ten!
Ready or not,
here I come!

Read me a story.

127

Penny

Penny said, "Hop a little.

Run a little.

Do not stop.

Jump a little.

Walk a little.

Hop! hop! hop!"

Away went Penny down the street.

128

A boy saw Penny.
He saw the bag, too.

The boy asked, " What do you have
in that bag, Penny ?
Let me see. "

" It's a surprise, " said Penny.
" I can't stop now. "

On went Penny
                down the street.

Penny said,

" I can run.

And I can hop.

I can jump.

But I can't stop. "

A girl saw Penny.

The girl asked,

" What's in that bag ? "

" A surprise, " said Penny.

" I can't stop now. "

On went Penny down the street.

Penny said, "Make a little run,
But do not stop.

Make a little jump,
And hop, hop, hop."

A woman saw Penny.
She asked, "What do you have
in that bag?"

"It's a surprise for Mother,"
said Penny.
"I can't stop now."

And on
she went
down
the
street.

131

Penny saw Mother.

" Do you want to see what I have ? "
she asked.

" It's a surprise for you. "

" A surprise ? " asked Mother.
" Do you want me to guess ? "

Penny said, " You can't guess.
Look in the bag, Mother. "

" A grasshopper ! " said Mother.
" Where did you get it ? "

" I made it, " said Penny.
" Do you like it ? "

" Yes, I do, " said Mother.
" I like the big yellow eyes.
Thank you, Penny. "

Dad came down the street.

" Come and see the surprise, "
said Penny.

" It's a grasshopper for Mother. "

133

" A grasshopper ? " asked Dad.
" For Mother ? "

Penny said, " It can jump,
          And it can hop.

          Make it go,
          And make it stop. "

Bozo

Mike wanted a dog.

" This house is too little
for a dog, " said Mother.

" But I have a name for a dog, "
said Mike.
" I can name my dog Bozo. "

" No, Mike, " said Mother.
" This house is too little
for a dog. "

Mike saw a frog in the park.
He wanted Mother
to see it, too.

Mike ran home with the frog.
He said, " Look, Mother.
I got this frog in the park.
I will name it Bozo the Frog. "

Mother said, " A frog !
We just can't have a frog.
Take that frog out of the house.
We just can't have a frog here, Mike. "

Mike went out of the house
with the frog.

He saw a boy with a mouse.

Mike said, " Let me have the mouse,
and I will let you have this frog. "

The boy went away with the frog.
And Mike ran home with the mouse.

" A boy let me have this mouse, "
said Mike.

" See what it can do. "

Mother said, " A mouse!
I will not have a mouse in this house. "

" Bozo is a good name for a mouse, "
said Mike.

" This mouse likes the name Bozo.
It's just a little mouse. "

" No, Mike ! No ! " said Mother.

Mike ran to the pet store.
He saw some ants in a box.

" Mother will not let me have
this mouse, " said Mike.
" Do you want it for the pet store,
Mr. Park ? "

" Yes, I do, " said Mr. Park.
" Let me have the mouse.
And you may have the ants. "

" Thank you, " said Mike.

139

Mike ran home from the pet store.
He wanted Mother to see the ants.

" I let Mr. Park have the mouse, "
said Mike.

" And he let me have some ants. "

" Ants ! " said Mother.
" No, Mike ! No ! "

" They can't get out of the box, "
said Mike.

But Mother said, " No ! "

140

" Oh, Mother, " said Mike.

" I want a pet.

I just have to have a pet. "

" You do want a pet, don't you ? "
asked Mother.

" I guess we will have to get a pet
for you.

And I know just the pet you will like.

Do you want a little dog ? "

" I saw a little dog in the pet store, "
said Mike.

" I do want a dog, Mother. "

Mother and Mike went to the store.
They saw the little dog.

Mike said, " Come here, Bozo. "

" We will take this dog, "
said Mother.
" Bozo will make a good pet for Mike. "

" He came to me ! " said Mike.
" He likes the name Bozo. "

142

143

Mr. Cunningham

Pat said, " I don't want to be a boy.
I don't want to be Pat.
I want to be a man.
I'm going to be Mr. Cunningham. "

144

Mother said, " Come on, Pat.
It's time to go to the city. "

Pat said, " Don't call me Pat.
Call me Mr. Cunningham. "

Mother looked up in surprise.
She said, " Hello, Mr. Cunningham.
Are you going to the city with me ? "

Pat said, " Yes, I am. "

Mother said, " Look, Pat.
See the balloon man ? "

" Yes, " said Pat.
" But I'm not Pat now.
Call me Mr. Cunningham. "

" I will, " said Mother.
" Come with me,
Mr. Cunningham. "

Pat went with Mother.

They went in and out of some stores.

They walked and walked.

"Here's a toy store," said Pat.

"I want to go in and see the toys."

"Toys are for boys," said Mother.

"Do you play with toys,
Mr. Cunningham?"

" Mr. Cunningham is not here now, " said Pat.

" He went for a walk in the park. "

Mother asked, " Are you Pat now ? "

" Yes, I am, " said Pat.

" I want to see the toys. "

Mother and Pat looked at the toys.

They saw a toy for Pat.

148

At night Dad came home from work.
He said, "Hello, Pat.
Did you have a good time
in the city?"

Pat said, "Yes, I did.
But don't call me Pat.
I'm Mr. Cunningham."

"Where did you get the space ship,
Mr. Cunningham?" asked Dad.

"In a toy store," said Pat.

Dad said, " Boys play with toys.
Are you going to play
with this space ship,
Mr. Cunningham ? "

" I'm not Mr. Cunningham now, "
said Pat.

" Mr. Cunningham went to see
some people.
This is **my** space ship.
I'm going to play with it. "

150

Mother said, " It's time to eat.
I made something Pat likes.
Is he here now ? "

" Yes, I'm here, " said Pat.
" Mr. Cunningham went away. "

" Good ! " said Mother.
" Dad and I like Mr. Cunningham.
But we want Pat to eat here. "

151

What Is in the Tree?

tale   tape
tame
same
name

mane mare
mate
date
late

case cage
cake
fake
make

cape
cave
cake
quake
take

cane cape
came
shame
name

game
gave
gate
hate
late

Reinforcing decoding: Ask the children to read "up the tree" and "out the limb."

152

Can You Guess What I Have?

It is good to eat.

You make it

from something in a box.

It is red, green, or yellow.

It shakes and quakes.

It is something you need

to play a game.

It is white.

You can hit it.

It may hit you!

This is a tame animal.

It is not as big as some

dogs.

It is white or brown.

It likes to eat green things.

You may hide something

in this bag.

What can you say to help

the boys and girls guess

what is in the bag?

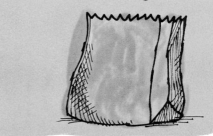

Word recognition and original thinking: Ask the children to read each of the riddles aloud and guess what is in the bag.

Go down
the Path

him
Jim
trim
am
ham
jam
Sam
whip
wheel
when

frame
Fran
Fred
free

stick
still
step
stem
stack
state
shine
she
sheet
sheep

shave
shake
shade
she'll

Reinforcing decoding: Have the words read from the top of the page to the end of the path.

154

OLD TALES

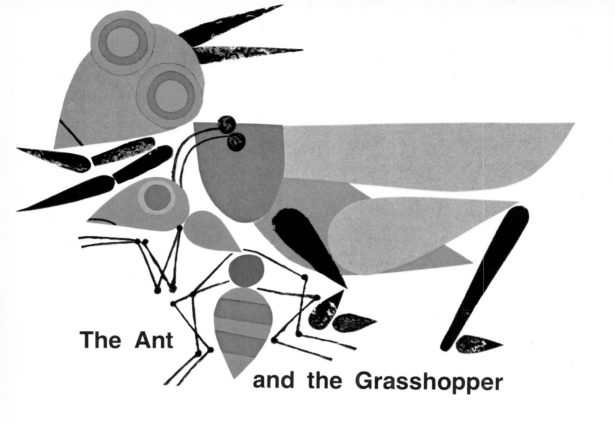

The Ant and the Grasshopper

"Hello, little ant," said a grasshopper.
"Will you come and play with me?
I will hide in the grass,
and you can look for me there."

The ant said, "You can hide
in the grass.
But I can't look for you there.
I have work to do."

156

" Don't work, " said the grasshopper.

" When do you play, little ant ? "

" I don't have time to play, "
said the ant.

" I'm looking for food.

I'm going to put the food away.

And when the snow comes,
I will still have food to eat. "

" Work away ! " said the grasshopper.

" I'm going to play now. "

And away he went in the grass.

The ant was still working.

She called, " You can play,
but I will work.

And I will have food to eat
when the snow comes. "

The snow came
in the night.

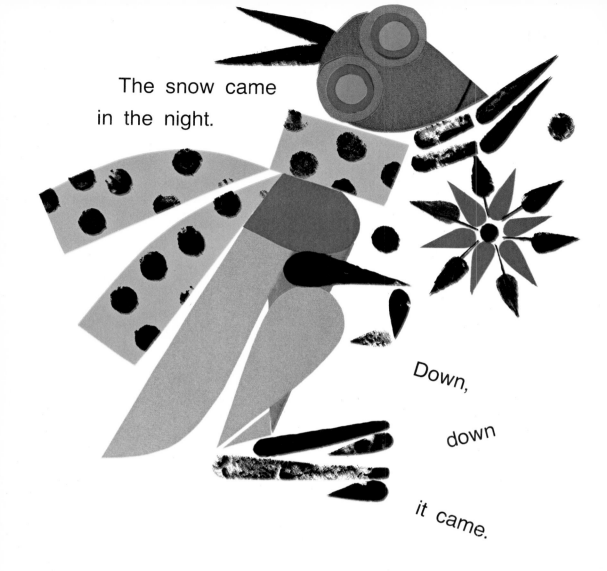

Down,

down

it came.

When the grasshopper saw the snow,
he said, "What am I going to do?
I can't play now.
I want some food, but what can I eat?"

The ant saw the grasshopper in the snow.

She called, " What are you doing there ?

Are you looking for something ? "

" Yes, I am, " said the grasshopper.

" I'm looking for you.

Help me, little ant.

Let me have something to eat. "

159

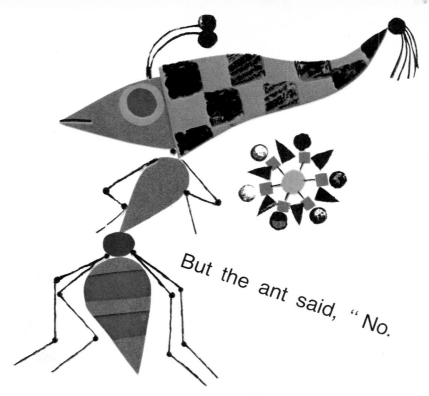

But the ant said, " No.

You played when I worked.

You didn't work, Grasshopper. "

And away she went.

" Stop ! " called the grasshopper.

" Don't go away. "

He called and called,

but the ant still did not stop.

And the grasshopper walked away.

On and on he went in the snow.

In the Country

The city mouse wanted to see
the country mouse.

"I know what I can do," he said.
"I'm going to the country.
I will surprise Country Mouse."

Away went the city mouse.
He ran and ran, and at last
he came to the country.

City Mouse called,

"Country Mouse!
Where are you?"

"Here I am," said Country Mouse.
"Did you come to see me?"

City Mouse said, "Yes, I did.
I ran all the way from the city.
And at last I'm here."

"What can I do for you?"
asked Country Mouse.

162

" Can I have some food ? "
asked City Mouse.

" I did not find a thing to eat
on the way. "

Country Mouse said, " Follow me,
and we will get something to eat. "

Then away went Country Mouse.
And away went City Mouse.

163

Country Mouse said, " Here we are !
Eat away, City Mouse. "

City Mouse wanted to eat.
But he did not like the food.

" You are not eating, "
said Country Mouse.
" Why don't you eat with me ? "

" I can't, " said City Mouse.
" I don't like this food.
Why do you eat it, Country Mouse ? "

164

Country Mouse looked surprised.

He said, " This is all the food
I have.

When a mouse lives in the country,
he eats country food. "

" Why do you live in the country ? "
asked City Mouse.

" Why don't you come home with me ?
I know you will like city food. "

" I don't know the way, " said Country Mouse.
" But I will follow you. "

Then away they went.

In the City

City Mouse and Country Mouse
ran up hill and down hill.

At last they were in the city.

" I know where we can get some food, "
said City Mouse.

" Follow me. "

" I will, " said Country Mouse.

" At last we are here, "
said City Mouse.

" We will go into this house.
The people will be in bed. "

" Do people live here ? "
asked Country Mouse.

" I don't like people ! "

City Mouse said, " It's night,
and the people are in bed.

They can't see you.
Come with me. "

And he went into the house.

Country Mouse went into the house, too.

He looked for City Mouse,

and he called, "Where are you?"

"Here I am," said City Mouse.

"Jump up here with me."

When Country Mouse jumped,

he saw some food.

" Eat away ! " said City Mouse.
" You will like this food. "

Country Mouse said, " I do like it.
I may not go back to the country. "

City Mouse said, " Don't go back !
You can live here with me. "

When they were eating,
City Mouse saw something big.
He said, " Run ! Run, Country Mouse.
And don't stop. "

Away went City Mouse.
And away went Country Mouse.
They ran out of the house.

170

City Mouse called, " Come back,
Country Mouse !

There is no danger now.

The cat went back into the house. "

But Country Mouse did not stop.

He called, " No, I don't like to live
where there is danger.

I'm going home. "

Country Mouse ran up a hill
and into the country.

When he got home he said,
" At last I can stop!
I will not go back to the city.
Not where the cat is!
I will eat country food,
and City Mouse can live in danger. "

THE THREE BILLY GOATS GRUFF

Once there were three Billy Goats,
and the name of the three goats was Gruff.

There was Little Billy Goat Gruff,

and **Big** Billy Goat Gruff,

and **Big, Big** Billy Goat Gruff.

The three Billy Goats Gruff
wanted to go up the hill
to eat some green grass.

But on the way up
was a bridge.
And under the bridge
lived a troll,

a **big,** old troll !

174

Little Billy Goat Gruff
walked on the bridge.

Trip, trap! Trip, trap!

went the bridge.

" Who's that walking on my bridge ? "
asked the troll.

" It is I, Little Billy Goat Gruff.
I'm going up the hill to eat
some green grass, " said the little goat.

175

" You can't walk on my bridge, "
said the troll.

" I'm going to eat you up ! "

Little Billy Goat Gruff said,
" Oh, no ! Don't eat me.
I'm just a little billy goat.
Wait for Big Billy Goat. "

The troll did wait.
He waited for Big Billy Goat.

176

Then **Big** Billy Goat walked on the bridge.

Trip, trap! Trip, trap!

went the bridge.

" Who's that walking on my bridge ? "
asked the troll.

" It is I, **Big** Billy Goat Gruff.
I'm going up the hill to eat
some green grass, " said the big billy goat.

" You can't walk on my bridge, "
said the troll.

" I'm going to eat you up ! "

Big Billy Goat Gruff said,
" Oh, no ! Don't eat me.
I'm just a big billy goat.
Wait for Big, Big, Billy Goat. "

The troll did wait.
He waited for Big, Big Billy Goat.

Then **Big, Big** Billy Goat Gruff
walked on the bridge.

Trip, trap! Trip, trap! Trip, trap!
went the bridge.

" Who's that walking on my bridge ? "
asked the troll.

" It is I ! " said the **big, big** billy goat.

" I'm going to eat you ! "
said the troll.
" **You** are the goat
I'm waiting for. "

Then up
on the bridge
went the troll.

He ran at
Big, Big Billy Goat.

But **Big, Big** Billy Goat
ran at the troll.

And down went the troll
from the bridge. Down,

down,

down.

Trip, trap! Trip, trap! Trip, trap!

Now the three billy goats
can go up the hill to eat grass.

There is no troll under the bridge
to stop them.

Stories We Read

The Three
Billy Goats
Gruff

Peter and the Wolf

182

Cinderella

Jack and the Beanstalk

The Little Red Hen

183

The Giant

I used to have a dream
long ago
about a giant
tall as a tree.

He came to the door
and said " Come, "
holding his hand to me.

I never went
but now that I'm bigger
I wish I had.
He may have been a friendly giant
and I made him sad.

Charlotte Zolotow

What's in the Middle?

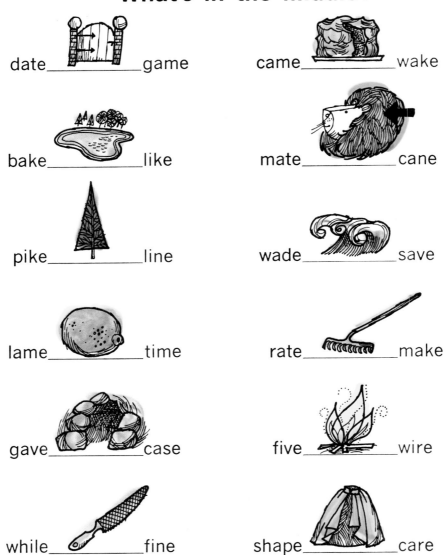

date _____ game

came _____ wake

bake _____ like

mate _____ cane

pike _____ line

wade _____ save

lame _____ time

rate _____ make

gave _____ case

five _____ wire

while _____ fine

shape _____ care

Reinforcing decoding: Ask the children to read the first and last words in each puzzle, and use these words to write on the board the word that is pictured between them.

Old Tales—New Tales

"Hello, little ant,"
said a grasshopper.
"Will you come
and play with me?"

The ant said, "Yes, I will play.
I do not like to work."

The giant came to the door
and said, "Come,"
holding his hand out to me.

And I went with him.

Country Mouse said,
"Here we are! Eat away,
City Mouse."

City Mouse wanted to eat.
He liked all the food.

"You are eating all the food,"
said Country Mouse.

"Why don't you stop eating?"

"Who's that walking
on my bridge?" asked the troll.

"It is I, Little Billy Goat Gruff.
I'm going up the hill
to eat some green grass,"
said the little goat.

"Wait, I'll go with you,"
said the troll.

Original thinking: Let the children read the "new tales" aloud and tell how they differ from the old tales. They may tell the rest of each "new tale."

This and That

I like

a little of this

and

a little of that.

I like

white sheep

green grass

blue sky

good sleep.

I like

the garden path

red balloons

purple grapes

a good bath.

I like

a big grin

a funny hat

a black cat

a pretty pin.

I like

a little of this

and

a little of that.

Reinforcing Decoding: Have the children try to read the verses. They should be able to decode most of the words on this page.

188

HOME FOR A BUNNY

"Spring, Spring, Spring!"
sang the robin.

"Spring, Spring, Spring!"
sang the frog.

"Spring!"
said the groundhog.

It was Spring.

In the Spring a bunny
came down the road.
He was going to find
a home of his own.
A home for a bunny,
A home of his own,
Under a rock,
Under a stone,
Under a log,
Or under the ground.
Where would a bunny find a home ?

" Where is your home ? "
he asked the robin.

" Here, here, here, "
sang the robin.

" Here in this nest is my home. "

" Here, here, here, "
sang the little robins.

" Here is our home. "

" Not for me, " said the bunny.

" I would fall out of a nest.

I would fall on the ground. "

So he went on looking for a home.

"Where is your home?"
he asked the frog.

" Wog, wog, wog, "
sang the frog.
  " Wog, wog, wog,
  Under the water,
  Down in the bog. "

  " Not for me, "
said the bunny.
  " Under the water,
  I would drown in a bog. "

So he went on
looking for a home.
"Where do you live?"
he asked the groundhog.

" In a log, "
said the groundhog.

" May I come in ? "
said the bunny.

" No, you can't come in my log, "
said the groundhog.

So the bunny went down the road.

Down the road

and down the road he went.

He was going to find

a home of his own.

A home for a bunny,

A home of his own,

Under a rock

Or a log

Or a stone.

Where would a bunny find a home?

Down the road

and down the road

and down the road

he went, until—

He met a bunny.

" Where is your home ? "
he asked the bunny.

" Here, " said the bunny.

" Here is my home.

Under this rock,

Under this stone,

Down under the ground,

Here is my home. "

" May I come in ? "
said the bunny.

" Yes, " said the bunny.

And so he did.

And that was his home.

• New Words in This Book •

The following new words are presented in *May I Come In?*, Level Five, Reading 360. Words printed in regular type are new basic words. Those underlined are enrichment words, and those printed in color are new words that pupils can decode independently.

UNIT I

page
- 6 work
  working
  doing
- 7 logs
- 8 helping
- 9 on
- 10 live
- 14 snow
  find
  Pat
  looking
- 15 food
  here's
- 16 put
- 17 tree
  finds
- 18 eating
- 19 raccoon
  he's

surprised
- 20 home
- 21 now
  follow
  down
- 22 up
  going
- 25 know
  tracks
- 29 made
- 30 danger
  some
  fawn
  bear
- 31 frog

UNIT 2

- 37 city
- 38 new
  boots

James
have
- 41 Penny
- 42 balloon
  thank
  looked
  comes
- 43 my
  red
- 44 went
  where
- 45 Jet
- 46 she
- 47 asked
- 49 saw
- 51 purple
  may
- 52 policeman
  lost
  Dandy
  I'm
- 53 oh

206

Pete
she's
56 machine
street
Ken
57 house
let's
Ken's
58 boxes
houses
59 Mop
60 worked
helped
62 buildings
take
men
64 finish
65 people
66 machines
that
these
pencil
sharpener
opener
telephone
dial
67 elevator
ramp

UNIT 3

71 all
fun
72 Mr.
sleep
cow
moo-oo
ma-a-a
quack
74 walk
75 walked
sleeping
76 cars
79 Carlo
Babbit
bed
82 out
of
84 without
was
wanted
85 jumped
88 space
Nog
Doodle
ship
89 Wig
91 things

bugs
92 yellow
eyes
94 imagine
hen
pen
cat
bat
pig
think
96 town
signs
Pine's
Pine
97 mayor
98 green
100 glasses
that's
102 got
103 were
mixed
109 fix
fixed

UNIT 4

115 girls
116 when

207

DEFGHIJ   7654321   PRINTED IN THE U.S.A.